The Death Of Christopher Marlowe

THE DEATH

OF

CHRISTOPHER

MARLOWE

BY

J. LESLIE HOTSON

Ph.D. Harvard University

LONDON: THE NONESUCH PRESS

CAMBRIDGE: HARVARD UNIVERSITY PRESS

1925

Printed and made in Great Britain
for the Nonesuch Press and the
Harvard University Press by
R. & R. Clark Limited,
Edinburgh.

THE CONTENTS

THE ILLUSTRATIONS

THE INTRODUCTION

SELDOM *is it the good fortune of any scholar, young or old, to make so remarkable a find as that which Mr. Hotson modestly chronicles in this book, and the alert ingenuity that detected and followed the clue removes the discovery from the class of happy accidents. The mystery of Marlowe's death, heretofore involved in a cloud of contradictory gossip and irresponsible guess-work, is now cleared up for good and all on the authority of public records of complete authenticity and gratifying fulness. Every detail of the strange affair is vividly set forth on the testimony of eyewitnesses. Incidentally Mr. Hotson has unearthed many curious particulars as to the character and station of the man who struck the fatal blow. And finally he has added a chapter to the history of the poet's early life which of itself makes a substantial contribution to knowledge. It is a privilege to introduce such a book to the reader, whom, however, I must no longer detain on the threshold.*

G. L. KITTREDGE.

THE DEATH

OF

CHRISTOPHER

MARLOWE

THE LIFE AND DEATH of Christopher Marlowe make one of the few dramas in our history which satisfy Aristotle's definition of tragedy. There is pity in the violent death that cut down such a tall genius in its youth, and terror for the faithful in the reasoned denial of God of which men whispered that the man was guilty. For three hundred years the tragedy of Marlowe has aroused a widespread interest. Curious fancy has spun unnumbered webs of theory round about the meagre accounts which have come down to us.

To the world interested in Marlowe, the present study offers for the first time the only authoritative report which tells how, when, and at whose hands Christopher Marlowe met his death. But, before the documents are brought forward, it will not be out of place to recall the main recorded events of the poet's life.

Christopher Marlowe came into the world at Canterbury on or about February 6, 1564, son to John Marlow of the Shoemakers' Guild. Shortly before the boy's fifteenth birthday, he entered upon a scholarship in the King's School, Canterbury, at the quarterly stipend of one pound. Two years later (1580–81), after proceeding to Cambridge, he was elected to a scholarship on Archbishop Matthew Parker's foundation at Corpus Christi (Bene't) College, where he took the bachelor's degree in 1583–4 and commenced Master of Arts in 1587.

Going up to London, Marlowe attached himself to the Lord Admiral's Company, for which he composed the greater part of his plays. He enjoyed the friendship and protection of Mr. Thomas Walsingham, of Sir Thomas Walsingham his son, and of Sir Walter Ralegh; and stood high in the brilliant group of poetical wits of Elizabeth's London. He was accused, with some show of reason, of uttering atheistical discourse. He was not, however, convicted of the crime of holding atheism as a creed, although his appearance upon summons before the Privy Council in May, 1593, had perhaps something to do with the charge.

May, 1593, brings us to the very month of the poet's

premature death. Even in the perilous days of Elizabeth, the taking-off of Christopher Marlowe was notable for its tragic violence. Pamphleteers of a homiletic turn dwelt upon the awfulness of God's sudden hand upon this man who had ventured to doubt and deny. And in the course of the three centuries and a quarter that have gone since Kit Marlowe died, more than one writer has taken his imagination out for a canter over the story of his end. An account of the early reports published, and of some of the exploits achieved by the historian's fancy, will be not less amusing than instructive.

A proper beginning was made by Thomas Beard in his *Theatre of Gods Iudgements* (1597),[1] a cento of terrific obituaries which exhibit God as almightily vindictive. In Chapter XXV, Marlowe comes in for the following: "Not inferiour to any of the former in Atheisme & im-"piety, and equall to all in maner of punishment was "one of our own nation, of fresh and late memory, called "*Marlin* [marginal note: *Marlow*], by profession a schol-"ler, brought vp from his youth in the Vniuersitie of "Cambridge, but by practise a playmaker, and a Poet of "scurrilitie, who by giuing too large a swinge to his owne "wit, and suffering his lust to haue the full raines, fell "(not without iust desert) to that outrage and extremitie, "that hee denied God and his sonne Christ, and not only "in word blasphemed the trinitie, but also (as it is cred-"ibly reported) wrote books against it, affirming our "Sauiour to be but a deceiuer, and *Moses* to be but a "coniurer and seducer of the people, and the holy Bible

"to be but vaine and idle stories, and all religion but a
"deuice of pollicie. But see what a hooke the Lord put
"in the nosthrils of this barking dogge: It so fell out, that
"in London streets as he purposed to stab one whome hee
"ought a grudge vnto with his dagger, the other party
"perceiuing so auoided the stroke, that withall catching
"hold of his wrest, he stabbed his owne dagger into his
"owne head, in such sort, that notwithstanding all the
"meanes of surgerie that could be wrought, hee shortly
"after died thereof. The manner of his death being so
"terrible (for hee euen cursed and blasphemed to his
"last gaspe, and togither with his breath an oth flew
"out of his mouth) that it was not only a manifest
"signe of Gods iudgement, but also an horrible and
"fearefull terrour to all that beheld him. But herein
"did the iustice of God most notably appeare, in that
"hee compelled his owne hand which had written those
"blasphemies to be the instrument to punish him, and
"that in his braine, which had deuised the same. I
"would to God (and I pray it from my heart) that all
"Atheists in this realme, and in all the world beside,
"would by the remembrance and consideration of this
"example, either forsake their horrible impietie, or that
"they might in like manner come to destruction: and
"so that abominable sinne which so flourisheth amongst
"men of greatest name, might either be quite extin-
"guished and rooted out, or at least smothered and kept
"vnder, that it durst not shew it head any more in the
"worlds eye."

This version was abridged by Edmund Rudierde in *The Thunderbolt of Gods Wrath against Hard-Hearted and stiffe-necked sinners* (1618), Chapter XXII:

"We read of one *Marlin*, a *Cambridge* Scholler, who was "a Poet, and a filthy Play-maker, this wretch accounted "that meeke seruant of God *Moses* to be but a Coniurer, "and our sweete Sauiour but a seducer and a deceiuer of "the people. But harken yee braine-sicke and prophane "Poets, and Players, that bewitch idle eares with foolish "vanities: what fell vpon this prophane wretch, hauing "a quarrell against one whom he met in a streete in Lon- "don, and would haue stabd him: But the partie per- "ceiuing his villany preuented him with catching his "hand, and turning his owne dagger into his braines, "and so blaspheming and cursing, he yeelded vp his "stinking breath: marke this yee Players, that liue by "making fooles laugh at sinne and wickednesse."

Francis Meres also used Beard's relation in his *Palladis Tamia* (1598):

"As *Iodelle*, a French tragical poet beeing an Epicure, "and an Atheist, made a pitifull end: so our tragicall "poet *Marlow* for his Epicurisme and Atheisme had a "tragicall death; you may read of this *Marlow* more at "large in the *Theatre of Gods iudgments*, in the 25. "chapter entreating of Epicures and Atheists."

To this, Meres added a few details, drawn, apparently, from contemporary gossip:

"As the poet *Lycophron* was shot to death by a certain "riual of his: so *Christopher Marlow* was stabd to death

"by a bawdy Seruing man, a riuall of his in his lewde
"loue."

. The report of Marlowe's lewdness, with which Meres
had fattened his account, seemed so pleasing and plausible to Anthony à Wood, who was writing his *Athenae
Oxonienses* (1691) almost a century later, that he added
it (somewhat heightened, it is true) to his copy of Beard's
classic narrative:

"But see the end of this Person, which was noted by all,
"especially the Precisians. For it so fell out, that he be-
"ing deeply in love with a certain Woman, had for his
"Rival a bawdy serving-man, one rather fit to be a Pimp,
"than an ingenious *Amoretto* as *Marlo* conceived himself
"to be. Whereupon *Marlo* taking it to be an high affront,
"rush'd in upon, to stab, him, with his dagger: But the
"serving-man being very quick, so avoided the stroke,
"that withal catching hold of *Marlo's* wrist, he stab'd his
"own dagger into his own head, in such sort, that not-
"withstanding all the means of surgery that could be
"wrought, he shortly after died of his Wound, before
"the year 1593."[2]

Meanwhile, in 1600, only seven years after the event,
William Vaughan had published a rather different and
more circumstantial story in his *Golden Grove*, which
Wood evidently had not seen:

"Not inferiour to these was one Christopher Marlow by
"profession a playmaker, who, as it is reported, about
"7. yeeres a-goe wrote a booke against the Trinitie: but
"see the effects of Gods iustice; it so hapned, that at

View of Deptford, in Kent.

"Detford, a little village about three miles distant from
"London, as he meant to stab with his ponyard one
"named Ingram, that had inuited him thither to a feast,
"and was then playing at tables, he quickly perceyuing
"it, so auoyded the thrust, that withall drawing out his
"dagger for his defence, hee stabd this Marlow into the
"eye, in such sort, that his braines comming out at the
"daggers point, hee shortlie after dyed. Thus did God,
"the true executioner of diuine iustice, worke the ende
"of impious Atheists."

For more than a hundred years after Anthony à Wood
the stories were repeated without any significant addition, and memory of Elizabethan times was grown
so dim in certain quarters that men even questioned
the fact that Marlowe had ever existed. But in 1820
James Broughton, the literary antiquary, on ruminat-
ing Vaughan's detailed account of the matter, conceived
the practical notion of writing down to the parson of the
church at Deptford to see if by any chance a record of
Marlowe's burial had been preserved there. He was surprised and gratified to receive the following reply:

*Extract from the Register of Burials in the Parish of
St. Nicholas, Deptford:*

*1st June, 1593. Christopher Marlow, slaine by Ffran-
cis Archer.*

A True Copy—D. Jones, Minister.[3]

While this discovery showed that Marlowe was indeed
more than a myth, and corroborated Vaughan's statement as to *where* the slaying took place, it added a com-

B

plication in the name of the slayer. Vaughan had named him as 'one Ingram', whereas from the burial register D. Jones, Minister, read 'Ffrancis Archer'.

With the tremendous growth of interest in the Elizabethan drama which the last century has witnessed, historians of literature have had good exercise on the circumstances of Marlowe's death. An excellent digest[4] of the scholarly fancy expended on the matter has been made by J. Le Gay Brereton, of which one or two extracts will serve to show the drift:

"Though his [Marlowe's] disgraceful life must have "brought him almost to the sink of beggary, he was so "foolishly ostentatious that, as Mr. Oliphant Smeaton "has recently been able to assure us, he maintained a ser-"vant—one Francis Ingram, a fellow whose character "was no better than that of his master. Mr. F. Meres "bluntly describes Ingram as 'a bawdy serving-man', and "we have Mr. Watts-Dunton's authority for calling him "a villain. His duties were various. The brothers Dido "define him generally as '*un homme en livrée*' and perhaps "Mr. Pinkerton means much the same when he desig-"nates him a lackey. M. F.V. Hugo and M. Mézières add "little by describing him as '*un valet*'; but Mr. Kingsley "distinctly tells us that he performed the tasks of a foot-"man, and Mr. Arthur A. D. Bayldon adds the informa-"tion that he combined them with the humble offices of a "scullion. Obviously he was a man of all work. At home "he probably cooked the dinner and washed the dishes, "and perhaps descended to jobs of an even humbler and

"more unpleasant nature. Undoubtedly he brushed from
"Marlowe's hose the mire of the London kennels, and
"sponged from his doublet the stains of grease and
"sack. . . .

"Marlowe was in love with a woman who played him
"false ('*comme Shakespeare, comme Molière, et comme
"tant d'autres*' remarks M. Hugo). His choice of an
"object for his contemptible affections was character-
"istic. M. Taine, in referring to the lady, uses lan-
"guage which we cannot permit ourselves to repeat,
"and Mr. Pinkerton and others merely indulge in less
"offensive synonyms. The brothers Dido discreetly
"suggest that she was '*une fille de basse condition*'. Can
"we be surprised that the infidel roué had a rival?
"His rival was Francis Ingram. . . .

"We may surmise that, one day towards the end of
"May, 1593, Ingram had plotted to meet his stolen
"lady-love at a tavern in Deptford—rather a low-class
"tavern. '*Un mauvais lieu*,' cries M. Hugo; '*Un mau-
"vais lieu*,' corroborates M. Mézières; and M. Texte
"re-echoes the charge, '*Un mauvais lieu*'. A British
"jury must agree that on such a point the evidence of
"three Frenchmen is invaluable. Mr. Pinkerton brands
"the establishment with a very unpleasant name. At any
"rate the house was hardly respectable. It was the kind
"of place where they sell bad beer."

Novelists and playwrights have not been tardier than
the diligent historians in seizing their opportunity.
Stories and plays on Marlowe and his lamentable exit

have flowed from their pens in variegated colours of improbability. A baker's dozen at the least have been published, from Tieck's *Dichterleben* (1826), in which Marlowe is slain by Ingeram, a rustic Yorkshire footman, to Clemence Dane's *Will Shakespeare* (1922), in which Marlowe is accidentally killed in the third act, and Ernest Milton's piece (1924), wherein Marlowe receives a mortal wound in the Mermaid Tavern while killing the murderer of a pure and innocent girl. The unfortunate poet and his slayer have universally been regarded as fair game for invention.

Yet, apart from the frankly fanciful writings, no great harm would have been done to literary history if the scholars had at least been more careful to ascertain the name of Marlowe's slayer. For as a matter of fact the man's name as entered in the burial register was *not* Archer, but Frezer. Alexander Dyce, however, in his edition of Marlowe (1850, 1858), adopted the *Archer* reading, and he has been followed by the great majority of writers. Halliwell-Phillipps was apparently the first to think of examining the entry for himself. He read the name as *ffrezer* (that is, Frezer). Drake's edition of Hasted's *Kent* (1886), in the compiling of which many original records were examined, also reads *Frezer*. In 1898 a certain W. G. Zeigler published a theory of Marlowe's death which outdoes all others for unfettered whimsicality, entitled *It was Marlowe* (*sc.* who killed Frazer and wrote Shakspere under Frazer's name until he in turn was murdered by Ben Jonson in 1598). Zeigler

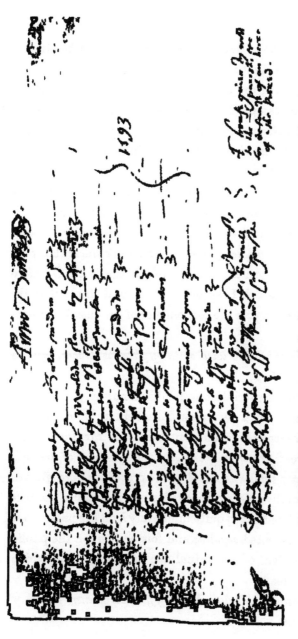

EXTRACT FROM BURIAL REGISTER OF ST. NICHOLAS CHURCH, DEPTFORD)

'Christopher Marlowe, slain by Francis Archer, sepultus 1 of June

gave another Deptford minister, one W. Chandler, as his authority for the *Frazer* reading.

In spite of the palpable jar between the 'Archer' and 'Frezer' camps, Sir Sidney Lee, writing on Marlowe in the *Dictionary of National Biography*, did not feel equal to throwing the weight of his authority on either side. He therefore left the question in the air, where it remains in the 1910 edition of the *Dictionary*. The most questionable treatment of this point, however, is to be found in John H. Ingram's *Christopher Marlowe and his Associates* (1904). In this work the author published an excellent facsimile of the page in the Deptford register (which I reproduce here), and transcribed the famous entry for the convenience of the unskilled reader as

Christopher Marlowe, slain by ffrancis Archer, sepultus
    1. *of June.*

In this transcription is exhibited not only a profound ignorance of a very plain Elizabethan hand, but also a reprehensible faculty for invention. Mr. Ingram not only read *ffrezer* as *Archer*,—although the *ff* of *ffrezer* is patently similar to the *ff* of the preceding word *ffrancis* and totally different from the *A* of *Alexander* in the next line, while the *z* is quite unlike any *h* on the page,—but coolly invented *sepultus* and foisted it upon the public in the place of the actual *the*. In a single line, which should read

Christopher Marlow slaine by ffrancis ffrezer; the ·1· of
    June

Mr. Ingram has achieved at least six errors. It is comforting to find that a Belgian scholar, M. Logeman, has laboured to repair the damage done to truth in the foregoing transcription by an expostulatory article in *Anglia* (1914).

The facsimile, read intelligently, at length disposes of the 'Archer' myth. There never was an Archer who had anything to do with Marlowe's death.

In the 'Frezer' camp, moreover, there is a strong tendency to gloze *Frezer* as *Fraser* or *Frazer*. This is a mistake. *Frezer*, which is pronounced to rime with *Caesar*, is a name totally different from *Fraser*, and one which has no connection with a Scottish clan. *Frezer*, or *Frizer*, is an occupational name, designating one who friezes cloth or covers it with a nap. Under *friezer* the New English Dictionary quotes passages which mention 'frizers and tesellers' (1485), 'Sheermen or Frizers' (1565), and 'drapers, cottoners, and frizers' (1871). There is no need or excuse for calling in a Scots clan to back the Frizers. They bear a name fully as honest and authentic as do the Teazles, the Drapers, or the Shermans.

When all that is superfluous and misleading has been cleared away from the problem, the data reappear. In the first place, it is certain that Marlowe met his death at Deptford in Kent before June 1, 1593; and in the second place it is clear that the only two names for his assailant which have a right to be considered are Vaughan's 'one Ingram' and the 'Francis Frezer' of the burial register. Of the two, 'Frezer' is doubtless the more trustworthy.

The foregoing considerations were in my mind during a recent search which I made (though for ends quite different) among the Elizabethan documents preserved in the Public Record Office in Chancery Lane. As I turned over the leaves of the Calendar of Close Rolls, my eye fell upon the name *Ingram Frizer*. I felt at once that I had come upon the man who killed Christopher Marlowe. Vaughan's 'one Ingram' was instantly clear as an example of the same habit of nomenclature which referred to Gabriel Spencer, Ben Jonson's adversary, as 'one Gabriel'; and I could only suppose (since the coincidence of two names so rare as *Ingram* and *Frizer* was in such a degree striking) that the 'Francis' of the burial register was a blunder. But the Close Rolls entry merely mentioned Ingram Frizer as a party to the transfer of a small piece of property, and gave me no clue to the crime.

Armed with a presentiment, I set out on the path which (as I feared) had been followed so often before—that leading toward some possible vestige of the official record of the Marlowe murder case. The printed *Inquisitions Post Mortem* yielded nothing, and I turned to the criminal records of the Court of the Queen's Bench for 35 Elizabeth (1593), in the hope that the case might have been brought to London for trial; but, in spite of an arduous and eye-wearying hunt, there was no indictment of Frizer to be found. The Rolls of the Assizes on the South-Eastern Circuit for the same year promised well, being covered with thick black dust, and abounding in Kentish gaol deliveries and criminal inquisitions post mortem; but Marlowe and Frizer were nowhere in them.

These cold faults on the trail were not a little disheartening. And since the Assize Rolls were incomplete and in part illegible, I was much afraid that the quarry was lost.

Yet, on casting about once more, it suddenly occurred to me that one of the numerous classes of entry on the Patent Rolls of the Chancery was *pardons*. If, as the ancient pamphleteers had said, the killing had been done in self-defence, then perhaps—and I turned to the original manuscript index and calendar of the Patent Rolls for 35 Elizabeth. A brief search yielded the following:

> *Regina xxviij° die Junij concessit Ingramo ffrisar perdonam de se defendendo,*

which may be put into English roughly as

> *The Queen 28th day of June granted pardon to Ingram ffrisar [sc. for homicide] in self-defence.*

This pardon was issued just four weeks after Marlowe's burial.

Although it was too late in the day when I ran the calendared entry down for me to see the Patent Roll to which it referred before the next morning, I had no doubt that the document would prove to be a pardon for the slayer of Christopher Marlowe. The only question was, how much detail would it give?

More than gratifying was it, then, when I opened the Roll on the following day, to find not only that it was indeed Frizer's pardon for having killed Kit Marlowe, but also that the pardon exactly rehearsed the terms of the Coroner's inquest, telling in detail the story of the fatal affray.

But that was not all. The fact that the pardon was included among the Chancery enrolments gave me a further clue. If the pardon was in Chancery, the writ of summons and a copy of the Coroner's inquest (upon the basis of which the pardon was granted) should be there as well. Yet I had already searched the *Chancery Inquisitions Post Mortem* in vain. As a last resort, I took up the (modern) manuscript calendar of the Miscellany of the Chancery. Here the documents listed, as the title gave warning, were highly miscellaneous both in nature and in date. They ranged from Edward I to Charles I and back again, and the only classification was by county. Nevertheless, by examining every item listed under *Kent*, I found at length what I wanted. The writ and inquisition were preserved, and in a legible condition. My search was now nearly at an end. One more document remained to seek: that is, Frizer's petition or bill to bring his cause into Chancery. Unfortunately such petitions were not so carefully preserved as the copies of proceedings upon them, and Frizer's prayer to the Lord Chancellor is not to be found in the collection of Ancient Petitions.

With this minor exception, there is here the complete record of the legal proceedings which followed the slaying of Christopher Marlowe. The findings upon oath of the Coroner's sixteen men, the writ of *certiorari* to summon the case into Chancery, and the resulting pardon.

Taking the case up in its order as a Chancery Proceeding, we have first the writ:

"Elizabeth dei *gratia* Anglie ffrancie & Hibernie Re-
"gina fidei defensor &c Dilecto nobis Willelmo Danbye
"Generoso Coronatori hospicij nostri salutem Volentes
"certis de causis cerciorari super quodam indictamento
"facto coram te de morte Cristoferi Morley super visum
"corporis eiusdem Cristoferi apud Detforde Strande in
"Comitatu nostro Kancia infra virgam iacentis mortui
"et interfecti vnde quidam Ingramus ffrysar nuper de
"Londonia Generosus indictatus est prout per recor-
"dum inde coram te residentem plene liquet Ac si idem
"Ingramus ffrysar praedictum Cristoferum se defend-
"endo & non per feloniam aut ex malicia praecogitata
"ita quod mortem suam propriam aliter euadere non
"potuit interfecit necne Tibi praecipimus quod ten-
"orem indictamenti praedicti cum omnibus illud tan-
"gentibus quibuscumque nominibus partes praedicte in
"indictamento illo censeantur nobis in Cancellariam
"nostram sub sigillo tuo distincte & aperte sine dila
"tione mittas & hoc breve Teste me ipsa apud Westmin-
"ster xv die Junij Anno regni nostri tricesimo quinto.

"POWLE.

"[Indorsed] tenor recordi in isto brevi mencionati patet
"in quadam inquisicione huic brevi annexata./.

"Responsio Willelmi Danby Coronatoris hospicij do-
"mine Regine"[5]

"Elizabeth by the grace of God of England France &
"Ireland Queen Defender of the Faith &c To our well-
"beloved William Danby, Gentleman, Coroner of our
"household, greeting. Wishing for certain causes to be
"certified upon an indictment made in your presence
"concerning the death of Christopher Morley, upon
"view of the body of the same Christopher, at Detforde
"Strande in our County of Kent within the verge[6]
"lying dead and slain, whence a certain Ingram ffrysar,
"late of London, Gentleman, is indicted (as by the
"record thence remaining with you it fully appears)
"And whether the same Ingram slew the aforesaid
"Christopher in self-defence, & not feloniously or of
"malice aforethought, so that in no other wise could
"he avoid his own death, or not; we command you to
"send the tenor of the indictment aforesaid with every-
"thing touching it and whatsoever names the parties
"aforesaid in that indictment are known by, to us in
"our Chancery under your seal distinctly & openly
"without delay, & with this writ. Witness myself at
"Westminster on the 15th day of June in the year of
"our reign the thirty-fifth.   POWLE.
"[Indorsed] The tenor of the record mentioned in this
"writ appears in a certain inquisition annexed to this
"writ./.
"Return of William Danby Coroner of the household to
"our lady the Queen."

Next we have the inquisition, returned by William Danby, Coroner of the Household, in obedience to the writ, into Chancery:

"Kanc./ Inquisicio indentata capta apud Detford
"Strand in praedicto Comitatu Kancia infra virgam
"primo die Junij anno regni Elizabethe dei gratia
"Anglie ffrancie & Hibernie Regine fidei defensoris &c
"tricesimo quinto coram Willelmo Danby Generoso
"Coronatore hospicij dicte domine Regine super visum
"corporis Cristoferi Morley ibidem iacentis mortui &
"interfecti per sacrum Nicholai Draper Generosi Wol-
"stani Randall generosi Willelmi Curry Adriani Walker
"Johannis Barber Roberti Baldwyn Egidij ffeld Georgij
"Halfepenny Henrici Awger Jacobi Batt Henrici Ben-
"dyn Thome Batt senioris Johannis Baldwyn Alexandri
"Burrage Edmundi Goodcheepe & Henrici Dabyns
"Qui dicunt sacrum suum quod cum quidam Ingramus
"ffrysar nuper de Londonia Generosus ac praedictus
"Cristoferus Morley Ac quidam Nicholaus Skeres nuper
"de Londonia Generosus ac Robertus Poley de Londonia
"praedicta Generosus tricesimo die Maij anno tricesimo
"quinto supradicto apud Detford Strand praedictam in
"praedicto Comitatu Kancia infra virgam circa horam
"decimam ante meridiem eiusdem diei insimul conuener-
"unt in Camera infra domum cuiusdam Elionore Bull
"vidue & ibidem pariter moram gesserunt & prandebant
"& post prandium ibidem quieto* modo insimul fuerunt
"& ambulauerunt in gardinum pertinentem domui prae-

* MS. quiete.

"*dicto* vsq*ue* horam sextam post meridiem eiusdem diei &
"tunc recesserunt a gardino *praedicto* in Cameram *prae*-
"*dictam* & ıb*idem* insimul & parit*er* cenabant & post
"cenam *praedicti* Ingramus & Cristoferus Morley locuti
"fuerunt & publicauerunt vnus eor*um* alt*eri* diu*ersa*
"maliciosa v*er*ba *pro* eo q*uod* concordare & agreare non
"potuerunt circa soluc*i*onem denarior*um* summe voc-
"*atum* le recknynge ib*idem* & *praedictus* Cristoferus
"Morley adtunc iacens sup*er* lectum in Cam*era* vbi cen-
"auerunt & ira motus v*er*sus *praefatum* Ingramum ffrysar
"sup*er* verbis vt *praefertur* int*er* eos *praelocutis* Et *prae*-
"*dictus* Ingram*us* adtunc & ıb*idem* sedens in Camera
"*praedicta* cum tergo suo v*er*sus lectum vbi *praedictus*
"Cristoferus Morley tunc iacebat *pro*pe lectum voc*atum*
"nere the bed sedens & cum ant*er*iori *parte* corporis
"sui v*er*sus mensam & *praedicti* Nicho*l*aus Skeres &
"Robertus Poley ex vtraq*ue* parte ip*si*us Ingrami seden*tes*
"t*a*li modo vt idem Ingramus ffrysar nullo modo fugam
"facere potuit Ita accidit q*uod* *praedictus* Cristoferus
"Morley ex subito & ex malicia sua erga *praefatum*
"Ingram*um* *praecogitata* pugionem *praedicti* Ingrami
"sup*er* tergum suu*m* existen*tem* maliciose adtunc &
"ib*idem* evaginabat & cum eodem pugione *praedictus*
"Cristoferus Morley adtunc & ib*idem* maliciose dedit
"*praefato* Ingramo duo vuln*era* sup*er* caput suu*m* longi-
"tudinis duor*um* polic*ium* & *pro*funditatis quartij vnius
"policis Sup*er* quo *praedictus* Ingramus metuens occidi
" & sedens in forma *praedicta* int*er* *praefatos* Nicho*laum*
"Skeres & Robert*um* Poley Ita q*uod* vlterius aliquo

"modo recedere non potuit in sua defensione & salua-
"cione vite sue adtunc & ibidem contendebat cum prae-
"fato Cristofero Morley recipere ab eo pugionem suum
"praedictum in qua quidem affraia idem Ingramus a
"praefato Cristofero Morley vlterius recedere non potuit
"Et sic in affraia illa Ita accidit quod praedictus In-
"gramus in defensione vite sue cum pugione praedicta
"precij xij^d dedit praefato Cristofero adtunc & ibidem
"vnam plagam mortalem super dexterum oculum suum
"profunditatis duorum policium & latitudinis vnius
"policis de qua quidem plaga mortali praedictus Cris-
"toferus Morley adtunc & ibidem instanter obijt Et
"sic Iuratores praedicti dicunt super sacrum suum quod
"praedictus Ingramus praefatum Cristoferum Morley
"praedicto tricesimo die Maij anno tricesimo quinto
"supradicto apud Detford Strand praedictam in prae-
"dicto Comitatu Kancia infra virgam in Camera prae-
"dicta infra virgam modo & forma praedictis in defen-
"sione ac saluacione vite sue interfecit & occidit contra
"pacem dicte domine Regine nunc coronam & dignita-
"tem suas Et vlterius Iuratores praedicti dicunt super
"sacrum suum quod praedictus Ingramus post occisi-
"onem praedictam per se modo & forma praedictis per-
"petratam & factam non fugit neque se retraxit Sed que
"bona aut catalla terras aut tenementa praedictus In-
"gramus tempore occisionis praedicte per se modo &
"forma praedictis facte & perpetrate habuit Iuratores
"praedicti penitus ignorant In cuius rei testimonium
"tam praedictus Coronator quam Iuratores praedicti

"huic Inquisicioni sigilla sua alteratim aff[ixe]runt
"Datum die & anno supradictis &c

"per Willelmum Danby
"Coronatorem."[7]

"Kent./ Inquisition indented taken at Detford Strand
"in the aforesaid County of Kent within the verge on
"the first day of June in the year of the reign of Eliza-
"beth by the grace of God of England France & Ireland
"Queen defender of the faith &c thirty-fifth, in the
"presence of William Danby, Gentleman, Coroner of
"the household of our said lady the Queen, upon view
"of the body of Christopher Morley, there lying dead
"& slain, upon oath of Nicholas Draper, Gentleman,
"Wolstan Randall, gentleman, William Curry, Adrian
"Walker, John Barber, Robert Baldwyn, Giles ffeld,
"George Halfepenny, Henry Awger, James Batt,
"Henry Bendyn, Thomas Batt senior, John Baldwyn,
"Alexander Burrage, Edmund Goodcheepe, & Henry
"Dabyns, Who say [upon] their oath that when a cer-
"tain Ingram ffrysar, late of London, Gentleman, and
"the aforesaid Christopher Morley and one Nicholas
"Skeres, late of London, Gentleman, and Robert Poley
"of London aforesaid, Gentleman, on the thirtieth day
"of May in the thirty-fifth year above named, at Det-
"ford Strand aforesaid in the said County of Kent with-
"in the verge, about the tenth hour before noon of the
"same day, met together in a room in the house of a
"certain Eleanor Bull, widow; & there passed the time

"together & dined & after dinner were in quiet sort to-
"gether there & walked in the garden belonging to the
"said house until the sixth hour after noon of the same
"day & then returned from the said garden to the room
"aforesaid & there together and in company supped,
"& after supper the said Ingram & Christopher Morley
"were in speech & uttered one to the other divers
"malicious words for the reason that they could not be
"at one nor agree about the payment of the sum of
"pence, that is, *le recknynge*, there, & the said Chris-
"topher Morley then lying upon a bed in the room
"where they supped, & moved with anger against the
"said Ingram ffrysar upon the words as aforesaid
"spoken between them, And the said Ingram then &
"there sitting in the room aforesaid with his back
"towards the bed where the said Christopher Morley
"was then lying, sitting near the bed, that is, *nere the*
"*bed*, & with the front part of his body towards the
"table & the aforesaid Nicholas Skeres & Robert Poley
"sitting on either side of the said Ingram in such a
"manner that the same Ingram ffrysar in no wise could
"take flight: it so befell that the said Christopher
"Morley on a sudden & of his malice towards the said
"Ingram aforethought, then & there maliciously drew
"the dagger of the said Ingram which was at his
"back, and with the same dagger the said Christopher
"Morley then & there maliciously gave the aforesaid
"Ingram two wounds on his head of the length of two
"inches & of the depth of a quarter of an inch; where-

"upon the said Ingram, in fear of being slain, & sitting
"in the manner aforesaid between the said Nicholas
"Skeres & Robert Poley so that he could not in any
"wise get away, in his own defence & for the saving of
"his life, then & there struggled with the said Chris-
"topher Morley to get back from him his dagger afore-
"said; in which affray the same Ingram could not get
"away from the said Christopher Morley; and so it
"befell in that affray that the said Ingram, in defence
"of his life, with the dagger aforesaid of the value of
"12d. gave the said Christopher then & there a mortal
"wound over his right eye of the depth of two inches &
"of the width of one inch; of which mortal wound the
"aforesaid Christopher Morley then & there instantly
"died; And so the Jurors aforesaid say upon their oath
"that the said Ingram killed & slew Christopher Mor-
"ley aforesaid on the thirtieth day of May in the thirty-
"fifth year named above at Detford Strand aforesaid
"within the verge in the room aforesaid within the
"verge in the manner and form aforesaid in the defence
"and saving of his own life, against the peace of our
"said lady the Queen, her now crown & dignity; And
"further the said Jurors say upon their oath that the
"said Ingram after the slaying aforesaid perpetrated &
"done by him in the manner & form aforesaid neither
"fled nor withdrew himself; But what goods or chattels,
"lands or tenements the said Ingram had at the time
"of the slaying aforesaid, done & perpetrated by him
"in the manner & form aforesaid, the said Jurors are

C

"totally ignorant. In witness of which thing the said
"Coroner as well as the Jurors aforesaid to this In-
"quisition have interchangeably set their seals.
"Given the day & year above named &c

"by WILLIAM DANBY
"Coroner."

Finally, the enrolment of the pardon.

"Regina perdona se   "Regina Omnibus Balliuis & fi-
"defendendo pro   "delibus suis ad quos &c salutem
"Ingramo ffrysar   "Cum per quandam Inquisicion-
                      "em indentatam captam apud
"Detford Strand in Comitatu nostro Kancia infra vir-
"gam primo die Junij vltimo praeterito coram Willelmo
"Danby generoso Coronatore hospicij nostri super vi-
"sum corporis Christoferi Morley ibidem iacentis mor-
"tui & interfecti per sacrum Nicholai Draper Generosi
"Wolstani Randall Generosi Willelmi Curry Adriani
"Walker Johannis Barber Roberti Baldwine Egidij ffeld
"Georgij Halfepenny Henrici Awger Jacobi Batte
"Henrici Bendin Thome Batte senioris Johannis Bald-
"wyn Alexandri Burrage Edmundi Goodcheape & Hen-
"rici Dabyns compertum existit Quod quidam Ingramus
"ffrisar nuper de Londonia Generosus ac praedictus
"Cristoferus Morley Ac quidam Nicholaus Skeres nuper
"de Londonia Generosus ac Robertus Poley de Londonia
"praedicta Generosus tricesimo die Maij vltimo prae-
"terito apud Detford Strande praedictam in praedicto
"Comitatu nostro Kancia infra virgam circa horam deci-

"mam ante meridiem eiusdem diei insimul conuenerunt
"in Camera infra domum cuiusdam Elionore Bull vidue
"& ibidem pariter moram gesserunt & prandebant &
"post prandium ibidem in quieto modo insimul fuerunt
"& ambulauerunt in Gardinum pertinentem domui prae-
"dicto vsque horam sextam post meridiem eiusdem diei
"& tunc recesserunt a gardino praedicto in Cameram
"praedictam & ibidem insimul & pariter cenabant &
"post cenam praedicti Ingramus & Christoferus Morley
"locuti fuerunt & publicauerunt vnus eorum alteri di-
"uersa malitiosa verba pro eo quod concordare & agreare
"non potuerunt circa solucionem denariorum summe vo-
"catum le Reckoninge ibidem & praedictus Xpoferus
"Morley adtunc iacens super lectum in Camera vbi cen-
"auerunt & ira motus versus praefatum Ingramum ffrisar
"super verbis vt praefertur inter eos praelocutis Et prae-
"dictus Ingramus adtunc & ibidem sedens in Camera
"praedicta cum tergo suo versus lectum vbi praedictus
"Cristoferus Morley tunc iacebat prope lectum vocatum
"nere the Bedd sedens & cum anteriori parte corporis
"sui versus mensam & praedicti Nicholaus Skeres &
"Robertus Poley ex vtraque parte ipsius Ingrami sedentes
"tali modo vt idem Ingramus ffrisar nullo modo fugam
"facere potuit Ita accidit quod praedictus Cristoferus
"Morley ex subito & ex malicia sua erga praefatum
"Ingramum praecogitata pugionem praedicti Ingrami
"super tergum suum existentem maliciose adtunc &
"ibidem euaginabat & cum eodem pugione praedictus
"Cristoferus Morley adtunc & ibidem maliciose dedit

"praefato Ingramo duo vulnera super Caput suum longi-
"tudinis duorum policium & profunditatis quartij vnius
"pollicis Super quo praedictus Ingramus metuens occidi
"& sedens in forma praedicta inter praefatos Nicholaum
"Skeres & Robertum Poley Ita quod vlterius aliquo
"modo recedere non potuit in sua defensione & salua-
"cione vite sue adtunc & ibidem contendebat cum prae-
"fato Χροfero Morley recipere ab eo pugionem suum
"praedictum In qua quidem affraia idem Ingramus a
"praefato Χροfero Morley vlterius recedere non potuit
"Et sic in affraia illa ita accidit quod praedictus Ingra-
"mus in defensione vite sue cum pugione praedicta precij
"duodecim denariorum dedit praefato Cristofero adtunc
"& ibidem vnam plagam mortalem super dexterum ocu-
"lum suum profunditatis duorum pollicium & latitudinis
"vnius pollicis de qua quidem plaga mortali praedictus
"Χροferus Morley adtunc & ibidem instanter obijt Et
"sic quod praedictus Ingramus praefatum Cristoferum
"Morley praedicto tricesimo die Maij vltimo praeterito
"apud Detford Strande praedictam in praedicto Comi-
"tatu nostro Kancia infra virgam in Camera praedicta
"infra Virgam modo & forma praedictis in defensione ac
"saluacione vite sue interfecit & occidit contra pacem
"nostram coronam & dignitatem nostras Sicut per teno-
"rem Recordi Inquisicionis praedicte quem coram nobis
"in Cancellaria nostra virtute brevis nostri venire feci-
"mus plenius liquet Nos igitur pietate moti perdonaui-
"mus eidem Ingramo ffrisar sectam pacis nostre que ad
"nos versus praedictum Ingramum pertinet pro morte

"supradicta & firmam pacem nostram ei inde concedi-
"mus Ita tamen quod stet rectum in Curia nostra siquis
"versus eum loqui voluerit de morte supradicta In cuius
"rei &c Teste Regina apud Kewe xxviii die Junij"[8]

This pardon rehearses the terms of the inquisition
almost word for word, omitting only the jury's statement that Frizer did not try to escape, and that they
did not know the amount of his property. It is necessary to give here only the final clauses of the pardon:
". . . And so that the said Ingram killed & slew Chris-
"topher Morley aforesaid at Detford Strande aforesaid
"in our said County of Kent within the verge in the
"room aforesaid within the verge in the manner & form
"aforesaid in the defence and saving of his own life,
"against our peace our crown & dignity As more fully
"appears by the tenor of the Record of the Inquisition
"aforesaid which we caused to come before us in our
"Chancery by virtue of our writ We therefore moved
"by piety have pardoned the same Ingram ffrisar the
"breach of our peace which pertains to us against the
"said Ingram for the death above mentioned & grant
"to him our firm peace Provided nevertheless that the
"right remain in our Court if anyone should wish to
"complain of him concerning the death above men-
"tioned In testimony &c Witness the Queen at Kewe
"on the 28th day of June."
From these documents the chronology of the case
emerges as follows: Ingram Frizer killed Christopher

Marlowe on the evening of Wednesday, May 30, 1593.
The inquest was held on Friday, June 1; and on the
same day they buried Marlowe's body. The writ of *certiorari* was issued out of the Chancery just two weeks
later—on Friday, June 15. Thereupon Coroner Danby
made his return, and Frizer's pardon was granted at
Kew on Thursday, June 28.

The members of the jury which viewed Marlowe's
body were not by any means all drawn from Deptford.
Only two Deptford men, William Curry of Deptford
Strand, and Giles Field of the Upper Deptford, were of
substance enough to appear on contemporary Lay Subsidy Rolls.[9] Others were impanelled from Greenwich,
which lay just across the Ravensbourne River from
Deptford: Henry Dobbins and Mr. John Baldwyn, who
lived in High Street East, Mr. Adrian Walker of Lime-
kills, Thomas Benden, and Wolstone Randall.[10] George
Halfpenny came across the Thames from Limehouse.[11]
In Woolwich I find a certain William Danby, who is
perhaps the same as our William Danby the Coroner.

One matter of some interest turned up on the Subsidy
Roll for East Greenwich (249/8). It will be recalled that
Thomas Beard's account (1597) relates: '*It so fell out,
that in London streets as he purposed to stab*', etc. So
patently absurd was it to have 'streets', in the plural,
that the passage was omitted in the 1612 edition of
his book; and in Rudierde's abridgment (1618) it was
altered to make an attempt at sense as '*a streete in
London*'. Ever since the slaying was shown to have

occurred at Deptford, writers have treated this statement with some scorn as an 'obvious error'.

Beard's inaccuracy, however, was perhaps not so great as it has been represented. For in the Subsidy Roll for East Greenwich one of the main thoroughfares listed is *London streete*. This *London streete* is reached from Deptford Bridge, and is but a few hundred yards from the scene of Marlowe's death.

Without doubt Beard wrote from hearsay. His informant had heard that Marlowe died in London Streete, East Greenwich, instead of somewhere in *West* Greenwich, *alias* Deptford. The printer added to the confusion by changing final *e* to *s*, making *streete* into *streets*. Despite Beard's inaccuracies, then, he is not such a blunderer as we have thought. A few hundred yards wide of the mark is better than three miles.

Now for the findings of the Coroner's jury.

A most important first consideration is that there were two witnesses to the killing, evidently friends of Marlowe and Frizer, who had been feasting with them. The finding of 'homicide in self-defence' in the case is based upon an examination of Marlowe's body, of the dagger-wounds on Frizer's head, of the dagger itself, and upon the testimony of the two eye-witnesses, Poley and Skeres.

Two courses are open to us: (*a*) to believe as true the story of Marlowe's attack on Frizer from behind, corroborated in so far as it is by the wounds on Frizer's head, which wounds must have been inflicted *before*

Marlowe received his death-blow, or (*b*) to suppose that Frizer, Poley, and Skeres after the slaying, and in order to save Frizer's life on a plea of self-defence, concocted a lying account of Marlowe's behaviour, to which they swore at the inquest, and with which they deceived the jury.

The latter seems to me a possible but rather unlikely view of the case. In all probability the men had been drinking deep (the party had lasted from ten in the morning until night!); and the bitter debate over the score had roused Marlowe's intoxicated feelings to such a pitch that, leaping from the bed, he took the nearest way to stop Frizer's mouth.

Beard and Vaughan differ from each other and from the official report in regard to the dagger. Beard says that Marlowe drew his own dagger upon his enemy, who, '*catching hold of his wrest, . . . stabbed his owne dagger into his owne head*'. Vaughan also tells us that Marlowe drew his own poniard on Ingram, but goes on to say that the latter, '*drawing out his dagger for his defence . . . stabd this Marlow into the eye*'. Neither of the old writers mentions the actual cuts inflicted by Marlowe on Frizer's head. The Coroner's record, on the other hand, explicitly says that Marlowe drew Frizer's dagger from its place at his back and had stabbed him twice before Frizer in the struggle got enough hold on the weapon to give Marlowe the final thrust.

We have seen that the quarrel which brought on the fight was a dispute over the reckoning. We cannot be

sure that Vaughan is accurate in saying that Ingram
had *invited* Christopher to this feast. No doubt there
was some serious misunderstanding about the pocket
which should disburse the pence. At any rate, the question of the score grew deadly. Word and blow followed
fast in those Italianate days.

Money is cause sufficient for a fight, without haling in
a woman. The object of Marlowe's imagined 'lewde loue'
is noticeably absent from the picture, both as a cause and
as a witness of the fray. In spite of the wishes of Francis
Meres and his followers, she must now be returned
with thanks to the fertile brain from which she sprang.

There is nevertheless a woman in the case: Mistress
Eleanor Bull, hostess of the tavern. While the Inquisition unfortunately does not give the name of her house,
and I have been unable to find any list of the sixteenth-
century public houses in Deptford, an entry in the
burial register of St. Nicholas, Deptford, gives us some
clue to Mistress Bull:

1590 April 9 Rich. Bull, gent.[12]

Deptford was a very small place. This Richard Bull,
gentleman, is doubtless the deceased husband of Eleanor Bull, widow. Now, since the probable owner of the
tavern had the title of 'gentleman', and there was a
garden adjoining the house which allowed perambula-
tion, the place was presumably not a low resort.

We return to a prime consideration. Who and what
was Ingram Frizer? From the Inquisition we know that
he was 'late of London, gentleman'. What then of the

'bawdy serving-man'? It was Francis Meres who started
that second snowball of legend on its career. What did
he mean by 'serving-man'? The greatest nobles of the
land were Elizabeth's household servants. William
Shakspere was servant to the Lord Chamberlain. The
questions put themselves: Was Frizer a servant? If he
was, whom did he serve, and in what capacity?

In my search for facts bearing on his life, I found that
Frizer, in all probability, was just as much a serving-
man as Christopher Marlowe, and that they both
served the same master. All this came out, however,
in quite a roundabout fashion. It is desirable to re-
arrange the data in order to make the case as clear as
possible.

Thus far, the earliest record I have found concerning
Frizer shows him as a man of some small means. On
October 9, 1589, he purchaséd the Angel Inn, situated
in Basingstoke, from the joint owners, Thomas Bo-
stock of London, gentleman, and William Symons of
Winchester, gentleman, for £120.[13] Within two months,
however, he had sold it 'for a competent sum' to James
Deane, citizen and draper of London.[14]

On the day that Frizer bought the 'Angel' (October
9, 1589), one of the sellers, Thomas Bostock, entered
into an obligation to him in the sum of £240. Bostock
failed to discharge his debt, and Frizer brought suit in
the Exchequer on June 18, 1591. After several delays,
he received judgment in Easter term, 1592, against
Bostock, with £4 costs.[15] Yet the debtor still de-

The Thames River
Deptford Strand
The Thames River

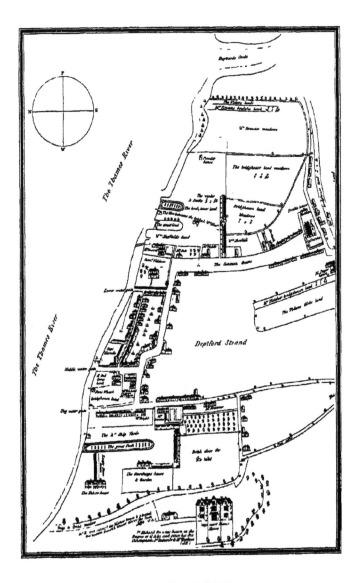

A Map of Deptford, 1623.

faulted, and Frizer at length obtained an execution against him in the Exchequer on May 30, 1595.[16]

The sums involved in these transactions show that Frizer, though perhaps not rich, was by no means poor. He no doubt made a penny or two by buying and selling small pieces of property such as the Angel Tavern.

In 1594, a twelvemonth after he had killed Christopher Marlowe, we find Ingram Frizer once more in the Court of Exchequer. It appears that on June 28 of that year one Thomas Smyth made over to him a house in the parish of St. Saviour's, Southwark, with possession for three years from June 24, 1594. Frizer took possession at once; but three days later, on July 1, a certain Edmund Ballard entered the house and drove him out. Frizer brought suit on October 17, 1594, in the Exchequer for recovery, and claimed £40 damages. He recovered possession, with £5 damages and 6d. costs [17]

In the 'Angel' transactions, and in the Bostock suit in the Exchequer, Frizer is styled 'of London, yeoman'. By the terms of the Coroner's inquisition, he was 'late of London, Gentleman', and in the Ballard case, 'Ingram Frizer, Gentleman'. Thus far there is no hint that he was in service to a master.

A long search through the voluminous 'Chancery Proceedings, Elizabeth', produced a suit in which Ingram Frizer was the defendant. The record consists of two membranes: the bill of complaint, and the defendant's answer. By ill luck, the right-hand side and bottom of both membranes have rotted away, leaving regrettable gaps in the dim script. A chemical wash and the keen eyes of an expert, however, got as much as possible from the documents, the sum of which I have printed in an appendix.[18] While the fragmentary nature of the documents prevents us from understanding the case fully, we may put together something from what is left.

Widow Anne Woodleff of Aylesbury, Bucks, and her son Drew accuse Ingram Frizer of practising, with the aid of Nicholas Skeres, a series of frauds on the said Drew, under the pretence of lending him ready money. Frizer's first device was to get a signed bond for £60 from Drew, against an assurance that he would lend Drew a similar amount in cash. When it came to the point, Frizer pretended that he had no ready money, and offered Drew instead some cannon, or great iron pieces, which he had on Tower Hill. These Drew was forced to accept; but he begged Frizer to sell them for him. Frizer made as though to sell them, and returned shortly after with £30 as the proceeds. Drew accuses him of never even offering the guns for sale, and of swindling him out of the other £30.

In the second place, Drew alleges that Skeres persuaded him to enter into another bond to Frizer, this time for 20 marks, under the pretence that such a procedure would lighten the burden of a similar debt which he (Skeres) owed Frizer; and that he (Drew) would get his money back at the end of the year, after

paying Frizer. That is, Drew should pay Frizer, who
would hand the money to Skeres, who would return it
to Drew. (I cannot profess to understand the ins and
outs of this devious transaction.) Drew, in good faith,
then, entered into a bond to pay Frizer twenty marks
within a year. It was all very well to involve young
Drew in these engagements to pay Frizer, but if the
young gentleman could not raise the money to meet
them on his and his mother's estate, it was plain that
he must be made to borrow it. To this end they induced
him to saddle himself with a further obligation of £200
'unto a gent*leman* of good worshipp [who was] the said
Fryser his then Maister'.

Keeping this in mind, let us see what follows. In his
answer to the bill of complaint, Frizer makes no
defence. He points out merely that Anne and Drew
Woodleff stand outlawed in a plea of debt in the Court
of Common Pleas, June 16, 1598; moreover, that Anne
stands waived on another plea in the Court of Hustings,
April 25, 1597; and ends by asking the Lord Keeper
whether he ought to answer the complaints of outlaws.

This bill and answer are all we have by which to judge
the rights of the case, since Lord Keeper Egerton made
no decree or order. Do the complaints of the Woodleffs seem to be *bona fide* statements of wrong? I believe
that they are such; for it is still harder to believe that
the Woodleffs trumped up the whole circumstantial
charge. I find, furthermore, that on April 30, 1596, the
Woodleffs sold to Ingram Frizer two houses and thirty

acres of land in Great and Little Missenden, Bucks,[19] and that Frizer re-sold the same within two years thereafter to one William Barton of Great Missenden.[20] This transaction adds to my impression that Frizer was making money from his dealings with the Woodleffs.

While I have not yet examined the Woodleff cases in the Hustings and the Common Pleas, I have followed the trail opened by Drew Woodleff's bond, or Statute Staple, of £200 'unto a gent*leman* of good worshipp . . . the said Fryser his then Maister'. The period indicated by the word 'then', according to the Woodleff complaint, is 'about fyve yeres nowe laste paste'; and 'nowe' must be some time after June 16, 1598, the date of the writ of *capias utlagatum*, to which Frizer refers. Subtracting five years, we are brought to 1593 or thereabouts. The problem was to find the bond into which Drew entered. Entries of Statutes Staple or recognizances of debt were made in folio books kept by the Clerk of the Recognizances. These books are now preserved with the Lord Chamberlain's papers in the Public Record Office, and are referred to by contemporary manuscript indices. A careful search yielded an entry,[21] dated June 29, 1593, by which Drew Woodlef of Peterley, Bucks, gentleman, was bound to Thomas Walsingham of Chislehurst, Kent, esquire, in the sum of £200 to be paid by July 25, 1593. A note shows that on Drew's default the debt was certified for settlement into Chancery. Here, then, is young Drew in a bond of £200 'unto a gent*leman* of good worshipp'. And the gentleman,

Thomas Walsingham of Chislehurst, is the patron of
Christopher Marlowe, and Ingram Frizer's master

We have thus arrived at a fact of the first importance
connecting Marlowe and Frizer.

So much for the illuminating Woodleff case. It has
shown us that Frizer was intimate with Nicholas Skeres,
who was present at Marlowe's death. Further, it has
led us to the knowledge that Frizer was servant to Mr.
Thomas Walsingham. Scholars have long been aware,
from the Privy Council summons of May 18, 1593, that
Marlowe was known to be staying at Mr. Walsingham's
house at Scadbury, Chislehurst. Everything, then,
points to an association between Marlowe and Frizer at
Scadbury as dependents of the same wealthy gentleman.

This hypothesis is strengthened by later documents.
Among the Signet Office Docquets I find the following
warrant, dated September 5, 1603:[22]

"Mʳ Frysar   "A warrant to the Chancelloʳ and At-
"Lease   "torney of the Duchie of Lanc*aster* for
                  "a Lease in Rev*er*cion to be made to
"Ingram ffrysar wᵗʰout ffyne to his owne vse and for
"ffortie yeres of landes ten*emen*tes and hereditaments
"wᵗʰin the survey of the said Duchie amounting to the
"yerely value of fortie poundes or therabouts."

An undated note[23] among the State Papers obviously
refers to the above warrant:

"After my hartie commen*da*cions. Whereas his Ma*jes*-
"tie hath long sithens directed warrant to you for a
"lease to be passed to Ingram frysar at the sute of the

"La: Walsingham, which lease you do now make some "difficultie to passe by reason of the Restraint for the "Entaile of his Majesties landes. . . . Forasmuch as "the same warrant was graunted long before the said "restraint his Majesties pleasure is not to make stay "thereof. These are therefore to require you to passe "the same lease to the vse of the said La. Walsingham "[marginal note: With any reasonable favor that may "be affoorded her] according to your warrant in that "behalf. Provyded that it be done with such con- "venient speed, as his majesties service touching the "saide Entaile be not thereby hindered.
"Sir J: Fortescu."

The lease was passed in December 1603:

"A Lease in Reuersion graunted to Ingram Fryser for "the benefit of the Lady Audre Walsingham for 40: "yeares of diuers lands parcell of the possessions of the "Duchy of Lancaster Rent per annum:—42ˡ¹ 6ˢ 3ᵈ."[24]

Lady Audrey Walsingham was the wife of Sir Thomas Walsingham (Marlowe's friend), and daughter-in-law to Mr. Thomas Walsingham, Frizer's former master. She was a great favourite of Queen Anne's, and was chosen in 1608 to be King James's Valentine.

From the above documents it is evident that in 1603, and later, Frizer was still connected with the Walsing-hams. Meantime, however, he had moved from London down to Eltham in Kent, much nearer to Scadbury. In a deed of sale,[25] dated in June 1602, Frizer is described as 'late of London yoman and nowe dwellinge at Eltham in the Countye of Kente'. Nine years later he was still living at Eltham, and appears on the Subsidy Roll[26] as one of the two certified assessors of the parish, being taxed one and fourpence on a small holding of land valued at twenty shillings.

Here we lose track of Ingram Frizer, though a trace of his name appears in the Eltham marriage register in 1629, when a Thomas Burton married Jane, widow of William Frieser.[27]

As for Nicholas Skeres, Frizer's friend, I have found little, and that little unsavoury. On March 13, 1594–5 he was arrested by Sir Richard Martin, Alderman, in 'a very dangerous company' at the house of one Williamson. He appears in the list as 'Nicholas Kyrse *alias* Skeers, servant to the Earl of Essex', and was imprisoned with the rest in the Counter in Wood Street to await examination.[28] On July 31, 1601, the Privy Council issued warrants 'to the Keeper of the prison of Newgate for the remooving of Nicholas Skiers and —— Farmer, prisoners in his custodie, unto Bridewell'.[29]

Robert Poley, who made the fourth in that fatal party at the Deptford tavern, is, I believe, identical with the Robert Poley employed by Secretary Francis Walsingham to spy out the Babington–Mary Queen of Scots conspiracy in 1586. Poley took an intimate part in the plot, as appears from the following letter[30] from Babington to Mary's secretary:

"Mr Nawe, I would gladley vnderstand what opinion "you houlde of one Roberte Poley whom I finde to haue

"intelligence with her Majesties accions, I am private
"with the man, & by meane therof I know somewhat,
"but I susspect more, I praye you deliuer your opinion
"of him/
"ANTHONY BABINGTON."

Even after Babington's arrest he had not learned
that his friend was a government spy. He wrote Poley
an incoherent and foolish note,[31] wherein he exclaims,
". . . Farewell my sweet Robin, if as I take thee, true
"to mee, If not Adiew bipedum nequissimus of all twoe
"footed creatures the worst . . ."
Yet some members of the Catholic party recognized
the deep part that Poley had played. An anonymous
letter[32] dated September 19, 1586, says "Theare is one
"Roberte Poole alias Polley [whom] the Papists gyve
"out to be the broacher of the last treason./ [They] rest
"perswaded that his committing to the Towre was but
"to bly[nde the] world after he had reveyled Babbington
"and his complices, [he in] troth consorted with them
"by the Counsells direction "
Poley, then, had been in Secretary Walsingham's service
as a spy. Frizer, servant to Mr. Thomas Walsingham,
was later accused, with Nicholas Skeres, of swindling a
young country gentleman. Skeres, servant to the Earl
of Essex, is heard of elsewhere only in prison.
Although we can hardly regard the three men who
ate the final feast with Christopher Marlowe as being
choice company for a 'pure Elementall wit', they were
certainly not his social inferiors. Marlowe and Frizer

MIDDLESEX
LONDON
Thamesis
PARTE
OF
Camberwell
Newington
Radriffe
Dagenham
Barkynge
Erith
Crayford
Bexley
Eltham
Bromley
Lathe

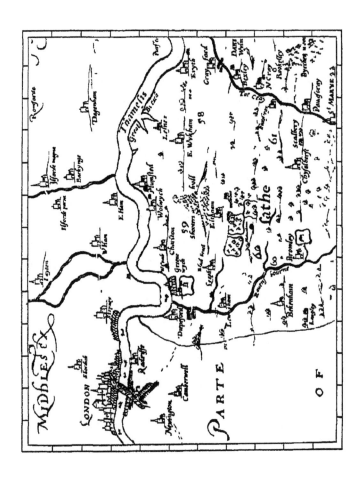

London and part of Kent, 1596.

must have known each other well, from their association at Scadbury. Such an intimacy helps to explain the quarrel over the reckoning. Companions quarrel much more fiercely than comparative strangers over such a thing.

{ 57 }

A   C E R T I F I C A T E

F R O M

T H E   P R I V Y   C O U N C I L

I N   F A V O U R   O F

M A R L O W E   ·

THE FORM *MORLEY* OF THE POET'S NAME,
which appears in the Coroner's inquisition, seems to
our eyes strangely.distorted from the familiar *Marlow*
found in the baptismal book of St. George's, Canterbury. Every student of Marlowe's life is nevertheless
aware that (even for those days of sportive spelling)
the variety of names he went under is notable. At
Corpus Christi, Cambridge, he was entered during most
of his college career chiefly as *Marlin*; and in his last
year of residence, most frequently as *Marley*. The spell-

ing *Marlow* indeed occurs nowhere in the University books. He took both B.A. and M A. as *Marley*; and we know from Sir Sidney Lee that it was as 'Christofer Marley of London' that he was bound over to appear at the Middlesex gaol delivery in 1588.

From *Marley* to *Morley* is no more than a step, and a step which the current pronunciation may have shortened. At any rate, we need not be discouraged by the spelling used in the Coroner's inquisition. On the contrary, the fact of its presence opens a new vista of possibility. Unnoticed records of the poet may be staring at us from familiar places, under a thin disguise of spelling.

An important example of this *ci-devant* blindness of ours is, I believe, the following entry[33] in the Privy Council Register:

"xxix° Junij, 1587   "Whereas it was reported that
"Lord Archbishop.   "Christopher Morley was de-
"Lord Chancelor.   "termined to haue gone be-
"Lord Threasurer.   "yond the seas to Reames and
"Lord Chamberlaine.   "there to remaine Their Lord-
"Mr Comptroler.   "*ships* thought good to certefie
     "that he had no such intent,
"but that in all his acc*i*ons he had behaued him selfe
"orderlie and discreetelie wherebie he had done her
"Majestie good service, and deserued to be rewarded
"for his faithfull dealinge: Their Lordships request was
"that the rumor thereof should be allaied by all poss-
"ible meanes, and that he should be furthered in the
"degree he was to take this next Commencement: Be-

"cause it was not her Ma*jesties* pleasure that anie one
"emploied as he had been in matters touching the bene-
"fitt of his Countrie should be defamed by those that
"are ignorant in th'affaires he went about/"

No comment on this extraordinary document is in
order until it can be proved that the Christopher
Morley here mentioned is the poet. At first glance such
a proof seems hopeless; for there *was* a certain Christopher Morley at Cambridge at about this time—a
scholar of Trinity. But a comparison of the years of
his degrees with the date of the document at once puts
him out of the question. Christopher Morley of Trinity
took his B.A. in 1582–3, and his M.A. in 1586;[34] whereas the Privy Council document is dated a twelvemonth
after the latter date, and but a few days before the
July Commencement, 1587, when 'Christopher Marley'
(our Marlowe of Corpus) took his Master's degree.[35]

It may be remarked in passing that the word *Commencement* used in a document of this period refers
exclusively to the University of Cambridge, and to the
academic exercises at which the full degrees—namely,
those above the degree of bachelor—were taken.

In reply to the obvious objection that our document
may be misdated by a year, it is only necessary to remem-
ber that a volume of the Privy Council Register is not
a loose collection of papers, into which such easy errors
might creep, but a continuous record book of proceedings, wherein entries were made almost daily. It is im-
possible to cast any doubt on the dating.

But, leaving the chronological proof out of consideration for a moment, what are the probabilities as between the two Christophers? Fortunately some small
light on Christopher Morley of Trinity has filtered
down to us. By an odd coincidence, it comes from the
same William Vaughan whose account of Marlowe's
death was the most accurate obtainable during more
than three centuries. Two years after publishing his
notice of Marlowe's slaying in the *Golden Grove* (1600),
Vaughan was travelling in France and Italy. Zeal for
Elizabeth and England moved him to write a letter[36]
from Pisa to the Privy Council containing a warning
against Jesuits. Of this letter the following is an extract, in part italicized:

"WILLIAM VAUGHAN TO THE ARCHBISHOP OF CANTERBURY,
  "SIR THOMAS EGERTON, SIR ROBERT CECIL, AND THE
  "REST OF THE COUNCIL.

"1602, July 4/14. I thought it the part of her Majesty's
"loyal subject in these my travels to forewarn the
"Council of certain caterpillars, I mean Jesuits and
"seminary priests, who, as I am credibly informed by
"two several men, whose names, under your pardon,
"according to promise, instantly I conceal, are to be
"sent from the English seminary at Valladolid, in the
"kingdom of Castile in Spain, to pervert and withdraw
"her Majesty's loyal subjects from their due obedience
"to her. I have therefore sent notice to some of you from
"Calais in France of some such persons, and of their

"dealing, the one of whom, George Askew, as he then
"termed himself, being made priest at Douay in Flan-
"ders, is taken, as I understand, and lies prisoner in the
"Clink. . . .

"*In the said seminary there is . . . one Christopher*
"*Marlor (as he will be called), but yet for certainty his*
"*name is Christopher, sometime master in arts of Trinity*
"*College in Cambridge, of very low stature, well set, of a*
"*black round beard, not yet priest, but to come over in the*
"*mission of the next year ensuing. . . .*
"Pisa, 14 July."

Over against this caterpillar Morley (or 'Marlor, as he
will be called') of a black round beard, and obviously
unknown to the Council, we may set 'Marley', later
known to be intimate with Sir Walter Ralegh and with
Sir Thomas Walsingham, cousin to Sir Francis Walsingham, the Queen's Secretary and member of the Privy
Council. Which of the two would be more likely in his
University days to obtain such a certificate from the
Council? Surely not the caterpillar of Trinity.

Likelihood is all very well, but identification of the
Christopher Morley named in the certificate with
the poet Marlowe does not rest upon a balancing of
probabilities. The proof is exclusive, made by point-
ing out the chronological impossibility of any other
explanation. 'Christopher Morley' here, as in the
Coroner's inquisition, means Christopher Marlowe the
poet.

Returning, we find that four facts emerge from the wording of the Council's certificate:

(*a*) Marlowe had been employed as an agent in State affairs, probably abroad, and had performed his commissions in a faithful and praiseworthy manner.

(*b*) Certain persons had defamed him (what they said maybe approximated by turning the Council's language inside out), ignorantly reporting that he was disorderly in his behaviour and indiscreet in his actions.

(*c*) Busy tongues had falsely given it out that he was to go to Rheims for a protracted stay.

(*d*) The Council wished him nevertheless to receive his degree at Cambridge in July.

The first two of these facts are of capital importance. All the official records heretofore discovered bearing on Marlowe have given him a doubtful, if not a definitely reprehensible character. The Middlesex Sessions bond of 1588 held him to appear 'at the next Gaol Delivery' for some unspecified offence. On May 18, 1593, he was summoned to appear before the Privy Council; and although the cause is unknown, it may well have been a charge of utterances suspiciously atheistical. The Kyd letters to Puckering, and the Bame libel both gave him a bad name on that score.

Here for the first time, then, is an official pronouncement in favour of Marlowe, during his lifetime, praising him, in the names of Archbishop Whitgift, Sir Christopher Hatton, Lord Burghley, Lord Hunsdon, and Sir James Crofts, for his good service to the Queen, and denouncing the ill talk which was being circulated by his enemies.

For the two latter items in the Council's letter (to wit, the denial of the projected emigration to Rheims, and the urging of his degree), doubtless the most plausible construction is the following. Marlowe's ill-wishers, taking the opportunity of his absence on State employment, had indulged in gossip about him; had represented to the University authorities that he was off to Rheims for good, and that for this and other reasons he should not receive his degree in July. Indeed the only probable cause for the drafting of such a certificate, it seems to me, is that Marlowe, returning to Cambridge from his employment in the spring of 1587, had met a cold reception. So completely were the authorities turned against him that to obtain his degree at all he was constrained to ride up to London and apply to the Council for their all-powerful support. With their certificate in his fist he returned and exacted his right from the Cambridge dons.

From Professor Moore Smith's valuable investigation[37] of the Bursar's accounts of Corpus Christi College it is plain that Marlowe's residence, during his last year at Cambridge, was quite broken. He was present for but half of his weeks in the second quarter. On Lady Day (March 25, 1587) his six years' scholarship came to an end, and for the last two quarters his name was omitted from the list altogether. Presumably, then, between February and July Marlowe was absent for some months

in the service of Walsingham or some other member of
the Council. Perhaps, as Dr. Moore Smith suggests, 'he
had resided a few more weeks before taking his M.A.
degree in July'.

What kind of business it was upon which the poet
had been employed, every one may imagine for himself
Since we know that he was intimate with the cousin of
Walsingham, it is possible that the work had something
to do with the secret services which were the Secretary's
province. It will be remembered that Robert Poley,
who was present with Marlowe, Skeres, and Frizer at
the Deptford tavern, was doubtless the Poley used by
Secretary Walsingham in 1586 to spy out the conspiracy of Mary, Queen of Scots.

T H E

C O N C L U S I O N

AS ITS CHIEF CONTRIBUTION, THIS PAPER
provides the authoritative answer to the riddle of
Marlowe's death. We know now that he was killed
by a companion of his, one Ingram Frizer, gentleman,
servant to Mr. Thomas Walsingham, in the presence
of two witnesses, Robert Poley and Nicholas Skeres
The testimony of these men before the Coroner's jury
was that Marlowe attacked Frizer from behind, and this
account was borne out to the satisfaction of the jury
by the evidence of two wounds on Frizer's head. Frizer
was pardoned, as having killed Marlowe in self-defence.
It is important to remark that he did not forfeit the
good graces of his employers, the Walsinghams, who
were friends of the man whom he slew.

E

Marlowe died instantly. This fact destroys most of
the interest in Beard's account, which builds on the
assumption that the poet died a more or less lingering
death, in the course of which he 'cursed and blasphemed to his last gaspe, and togither with his breath
an oth flew out of his mouth'. More material to literary history is the bearing of this fact upon the question of Chapman's continuation of *Hero and Leander*.
Marlowe's 'late desires', in accordance with which
Chapman took up the poem, cannot be regarded any
longer as a dying wish. After that mortal thrust, Marlowe had no time to make literary legacies. His 'late
desires', if indeed there were any such, must have been
communicated to Chapman in his active prime, before
any thought of sudden death had come to him.

In the light of all we have learned of Ingram Frizer,
his position with the Walsinghams, his property, and
his associates, it is curious to read again the passage
in Francis Meres's *Palladis Tamia* which runs, '*Christopher Marlow* was stabd to death by a bawdy Seruing
man, a riuall of his in his lewde loue'. Frizer was
occupied with a suit in Chancery when Meres published
this libel, or he might have made trouble for the ill-
informed and imaginative author.

The second part of the paper makes an important
addition to our knowledge of Marlowe's university
career, and to our ideas of how he was occupied just
before entering upon his life in London. We can now
picture Shakspere's great predecessor, supported by

his former employers, the Privy Council, wresting his master's degree from the cold and hostile Cambridge authorities. Most interesting are the terms of praise which, by his services, the poet earned from Archbishop Whitgift, Lord Burghley, Lord Hunsdon, and the other great officers of England. These men knew him as discreet and useful for the secret purpose of Elizabethan government. For us, such a reputation is hardly more to his credit than the accusation of 'blasphemy' is to his discredit. To praise a man as a faithful and effective secret agent is to throw little more light on his moral nature than to damn him for a freethinker.

APPENDIX

[*WOODLEFF* VERSUS *FRIZER*]

TO THE RIGHTE HONORABLE Sᴿ THOMAS
EGERTON KNIGHTE LORD KEEPER OF THE
GREATE SEALE OF ENGLANDE.

[No date.]

sheweth unto your good Lordshipp your dailie
Orators Anne Woodleff of Alisbury in the countie of Bucks
widowe and D   the saide Drue about
fyve yeres nowe laste paste wantinge mony made requeste
unto one Nicholas Skeres to be a   the
saide Drue his Bonde whoe knowinge that the saide Drue
stoode in greate neede therof and beinge perswad
         any reasonable Bargaine he shoulde under-
take ymparted the saide Drue his wante and meanes of
performance as afore   was by
ymployinge his mony to usurie with requeste to the saide
Fryser to helpe him the saide Drue to the some of
        saide Fryser (havinge a full purpose as by the
sequell of his dealings maie appere) to undermynde and
disceive the saide Drewe and kno
     into any unthriftie bargaine and havinge intelligence of
the uttermoste tyme when the saide Drewe was to use his
mony made   lx¹¹ made reddie
againste his tyme of need, uppon which   as aforesaide your saide Orator did in deede seale and deliver to the
         unto him of lx¹¹ at certaine Monethes
after But nowe so it is if it maie please your good lordshipp
that even at the very instante   use his
mony the saide Fryser toulde the saide Drewe that he had

noe reddie mony but he woulde deliver the saide Drewe a
commoditie   and for which he mighte
have threescore pounds (which was a certayne nomber of
gunnes or greate Iron peeces) which dealings of the saide
Fryser drave your saide   into   extremitie as that he coulde not tell what meanes to make for
mony but was inforced to take indeed what he coulde and
accepted therof, and because your saide   knewe
not what course to take for his mony for them entreated
the saide Fryser to helpe him to sell them for him as they
were worthe which the saide Fryser   woulde doe
as for himselfe so that your Orator woulde promise him to
be contente with what he shoulde doe therin (which he was
fayne to doe) and then the saide   Drewe as
thoughe he woulde sell them, and not long after broughte
        saide
your / Orator only Thirtie pounds protestinge that that was
all that he coulde at that tyme gett for
in truthe the saide peeces or gunnes were his owne and the
xxx^{li} he broughte his owne and never offered them to be
soulde at all but lett them remayne uppon Tower Hill
                and more which xxx^{li} only your saide Orator
was compelled by suche meanes as aforesaide to take for
lx^{li} his necessitie for use of mony was suche at that tyme:
Nottherwithall   saide Fryser (perswadinge
himselfe as it shoulde seeme that your poore Orator was a
fitt man for him to worke uppon in respecte of his wante of
monye withoute anie   science) farther
combyned himselfe with the saide Skeres and perswaded
with him the saide Skeres that he (in respecte of thaffeccion
which he perceived your Orator did beare
Skeres shoulde contrarie to the truthe affirme that he oughte
to the saide Fryser xx^{tie} marks in money and so procure
your saide Orator to enter into Bonde lykewyse

to paie unto him the saide twentie marks
protestinge that when he the saide Fryser should *Receive*
the same at your Orators hand he woulde paie it unto the
saide Skeres   effectinge the matche
aforesaide with the saide Skeres at that tyme also broughte
to passe And your saide Orators did then in deed seale and
deliver to the saide Fryser   marks for
payment of Twentie marks unto the [saide] Fryser within
one yere then nexte followinge in discharge of the saide
supposed debte of the saide Skeres of
ther was noe suche   by the saide
Skeres to the saide Fryser And farther the saide Fryser
knowinge and perceivinge the then   the
saide Drue had not   of his and his mothers
estate within twoe Monethes (after the saide former
matches) fell againe   saide Drewe to
gett   somuche mony more as woulde
make upp the foresaide sommes of lx^{li} and xx^{tie}
                              Orator   in his then un-
warie age And seemed willinge for effectinge therof) what
the saide   into a statute of cc^{li} unto a
gentleman of good worshipp   the saide Fryser his then
Maister with Dephesants   affermed that he had
speciall reasons to moove him to have the same and all other
                              maister wheruppon the saide Drue
as afore expected the resceipte of the somme of
                              beinge (therin included in this saide
                    lx^{li} and xx^{tie} marks but alsoe in
                              the lyke
                                        was of necessitie

ANSWER OF INGRAM FRYZER DEFEN-
DAUNTE TO THE

DRUE WOODLIFF AND ANN WOODLIEFF
COMPLAYNANTS.

acknowledginge anye the matters or
allegacions by the sayde Complaynants   or
declared Sayeth that the saide Complaynants or eyther of
them To the sayd   the Defendaunte
ought not by the Lawes of this Realme and due course
                              Defendaunt For that the sayde
Drwe Woodlieff by the name of Drue
                    att the tyme of the said bill exhybyted unto
this Court was and yet
Pleas of the Quene att Westminster in a plea of Debte att
                                        London the mundaye
next after the Feast of thappostells of Phill
                    majestyes Raigne as in and by the Records of
the proces of   Court of Comon
pleas remayneinge And whereuppon the Quenes Writt of
Capias utlaga   Court of Comon pleas
And hereunto affyled bearing Teste att Westminster the
sixtent   yeare of her heighnes
Raigne directed to the Sheriffe of Myddlesex to apprehend
            Drwe Woodlieff by force of the out lawrye
of the said Drwe aforesaide in the Plea aforesaide
                    more at large appeare and is manifeste
extent of Record And allsoe for that the said Anne Wood-
leffe   Anne Woodlieff late of London wydow
att the tyme of the bill exhibyted into this Court
            and standeth wayved in the sayd Court of Com-
mon Pleas of the Quene at Westminster in a plea of
            the Suite of John Gabrye and John de la F. . trye
in the Hustings of London the mundaye
        Feast of St Alphege Archbishopp in the nyne and

THE NOTES

[1] *The Theatre of Gods Iudgements. Or, A Collection of Histories out of Sacred, Ecclesiasticall, and prophane Authours, concerning the admirable Iudgements of God vpon the transgressours of his commandements. Translated out of French, and Augmented by more than three hundred Examples, by Th. Beard.*

[2] Quoted from the Second Edition (1721), i, col. 838.

[3] *The Gentleman's Magazine,* January 1830, p. 6. The find, however, was first published (obviously also by Broughton) in Kenrick's *British Stage and Literary Cabinet,* v. (January 1821), p. 22, over the signature 'Dangle, Jun.'.

[4] 'The Case of Francis Ingram.' Sydney University Publications, No. 5, pp. 3-8.

[5] Chancery Miscellanea. Bundle 64, File 8, No. 241a.

[6] The verge was an area of twelve miles round the body of the sovereign, in which the officers of the royal household temporarily supplanted the local authorities in their duties.

[7] Chancery Miscellanea. Bundle 64, File 8, No. 241b.

[8] Patent Rolls 1401.

[9] Subsidies 127/529.

[10] Subsidies 127/566, 125/305, 249/8.

[11] Subsidies 142/234.

[12] Hasted's *History of Kent,* edited by Henry H. Drake, 1886, p. 41.

[13] Close Rolls 1389.

[14] *Ibid.*

[15] Exchequer Plea Rolls 381.

[16] Exchequer Plea Rolls 396.

[17] Exchequer Plea Rolls 394.

[18] See page 69.

[19] Close Rolls 1520; C.P. 25, 38 Eliz., Easter, Bucks; Patent Rolls 1506.

[20] Close Rolls 1578; C.P. 25, 40 Eliz., Easter, Bucks; Patent Rolls 1506.

[21] L.C. 4/192, p. 267.

[22] Public Record Office, Index 6801.

[23] State Papers, Domestic, Addenda James I., xl. 46.

[24] Index 6801.

[25] Close Rolls 1711.

[26] Subsidies 127/566.

[27] Hasted's *History of Kent* (1886), p. 211.

[28] Historical Manuscripts Commission, Salisbury Manuscripts, v. 139.

[29] *Acts of the Privy Council*, ed. Dasent, xxxii. 130.

[30] Bodl. MS. Tanner 78/11*b*. A poorer copy is Ashmole 830/4.

[31] Bodl. Rawl. D264/1. A variant is B.M. MS. Add. 33,938/22.

[32] State Papers, Domestic, Elizabeth, cxciii. 52.

[33] Privy Council Registers, Elizabeth, vi, 381*b*. Public Record Office.

[34] *Grace Book Δ, University of Cambridge*, edited by John Venn (1910), p. 517.

[35] *Ibid.*, p. 514.

[36] Historical MSS. Comm., Salisbury MSS., xii (1910), 211, 212.

[37] Marlowe at Cambridge, *Modern Language Review*, January 1909, pp. 174, 175.

[38] Chancery Proceedings, Elizabeth. Bundle W.25, No. 43.

Lightning Source UK Ltd.
Milton Keynes UK
UKHW021342030921
389835UK00005B/1276